EUROPA ✠ MILITARIA

G000080599

WARRIOR COMPANY

Simon Dunstan

The Crowood Press

First published in 1998 by
The Crowood Press Ltd
Ramsbury, Marlborough, Wiltshire SN8 2HR

British Library Cataloguing-in-Publication Data
A catalogue record for this book is available
from the British Library.

ISBN 1 86126 191 8

Edited by Martin Windrow
Designed by Frank Ainscough /Compendium
Printed and bound by Craft Print Pte Ltd

Dedication:
To Roy Dunstan, bon viveur, gourmet, raconteur and inveterate smoker, whose unselfish contribution to society and his fellow men (and women) remains an example to us all.

Acknowledgements:
The author wishes to thank the following for their kind and generous assistance in the preparation of this book - as usual, the professionalism of the British Army shone through every encounter the author enjoyed with its personnel, and I hope that this is reflected in *Warrior Company:*

Michael Ball, MA, AMA; Sgt K.Blaney, R Anglian; Lt Col W.Cubbitt, Coldstream Gds; Mike Docherty, GKN Defence; Christopher F.Foss; David Fletcher and The Tank Museum; GKN Defence; Lt Col A.Groves, MBE, RGR; Lt Col R.Kemp, MBE, R Anglian; The Reading Room, National Army Museum; Sgt A.Rainey, R Anglian; Soldier Magazine; Jenny Spencer-Smith, BA, MA, AMA; Maj M.Steed, 1 Staffords; Lt Col J-D.von Merveldt; Media Operations, Wilton & Germany.

To the Officers and Men of 2nd Bn, Royal Anglian Regiment for their unstinting hospitality during various visits to the Combined Arms Training Centre at Warminster.

Finally, unless otherwise noted all photographs are courtesy of the Director of Public Relations Army, Ministry of Defence.

Warrior Company

Despite the widespread use of turretless tanks as armoured transports for infantry in the closing stages of World War II, the British Army did not pursue the concept of a fully tracked armoured personnel carrier (APC) in the immediate post-war years. The Army's extensive overseas commitments during the slow, controlled withdrawal from the British Empire absorbed enormous defence resources, and the principal requirement was for a wheeled APC to provide adequate protection for infantry deploying or patrolling over the great distances involved in many colonial campaigns. These carriers were not required to carry infantry into battle alongside tanks; most operations in the 1950s and 1960s involved either delivering them to jump-off points for foot patrols in undrivable terrain, such as that encountered during the Malayan Emergency and to a lesser degree during the Mau-Mau campaign in Kenya; or protecting them from close-quarter ambush during essentially road-bound internal security operations, such as those in Cyprus and Aden. This requirement gave rise to the 6x6 FV603 Saracen and the 4x4 FV1611 Humber APCs (the latter known as the 'Pig'). Both types were to soldier on into the late 1980s, notably on internal security duties in Northern Ireland.

It was not until 1959, following the Defence Review of 1957 - which advocated the withdrawal of British forces from East of Suez and the concentration of resources on the British Army of the Rhine (BAOR) in West Germany - that the Army formulated a requirement for an APC under the designation FV432. A contract for the design and development of four prototypes and 13 troop trial vehicles was awarded to GKN Fighting Vehicle Division. These were delivered on schedule in 1961, and in the following year the FV432 was accepted for service, initially as the Trojan. However, considerations of trademark infringement did not allow the use of this name, and the vehicle was known simply as FV432 throughout its career. Production of the FV430 series was undertaken by GKN Sankey and continued until 1968, by which time some 3,000 APCs and variants had been manufactured for the British Army. Many of the non-troop carrying variants will remain in service into the 21st century.

Plans for a successor to the FV432 had their origins in 1967 when the Ministry of Defence sought proposals for a future APC. Between 1969 and 1971 these were addressed by the Fighting Vehicles Research and Development Establishment at Chertsey in Surrey. At this stage the design featured a vehicle weighing some 30 tonnes mounting a two-man turret armed with a 30mm cannon and powered by a 750hp diesel engine - the same horsepower as the contemporary Chieftain Main Battle Tank which weighed almost twice as much. The vehicle was also to be fitted with an advanced form of protection known as Chobham armour, giving immunity against many infantry and battlefield anti-tank weapons; however, this feature was soon abandoned because of the high cost.

Feasibility studies continued throughout the 1970s in conjunction with industry, and many concepts were explored. Not the least of these was the facility for the infantry to fire personal weapons from the troop compartment, as allowed by several contemporary foreign designs such as the Soviet BMP and the German Marder. This was rejected by the British Army, but it remains an option on export models.

Following competitive tendering by industry, in 1977 GKN Sankey was selected as prime contractor for a proposed family of vehicles now designated MCV80 or Mechanised Combat Vehicle for the Eighties. Project definition continued until 1979, during which time the MOD also evaluated an American infantry fighting vehicle designated XM2 which was subsequently adopted by the US Army as the M2 Bradley.

In June 1980, following another competitive process, the MOD selected the MCV80 for full development by GKN Sankey Defence Operations. Further prototypes were built and extensively tested; four of these underwent trials in conjunction with the new Challenger MBT in the autumn of 1984 during Exercise Lionheart in West Germany. In November 1984 the MCV80 was accepted for service with the British Army under the name Warrior and the series designation FV510. Originally the British Army requirement was for a total of 1,900 Warrior vehicles at a cost of £1.2 billion, but this was reduced to 1,048 following the Defence Review of 1981. This was later pruned even further under 'Options for Change' - a euphemism for radical defence expenditure cuts following the collapse of the Soviet Union.

Into service

The introduction into service of Warrior coincided with a widespread reappraisal of British Army doctrine. For almost forty years BAOR had adopted a predominantly defensive posture to counter the threat

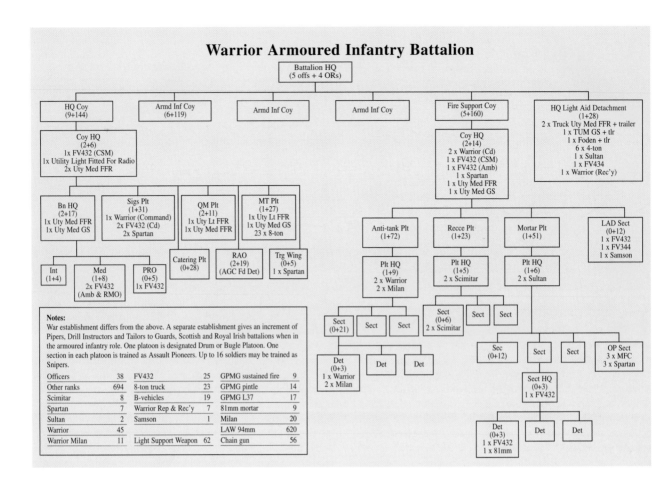

of the Warsaw Pact. WARPAC forces threatened Western Europe with a massive conventional onslaught designed to overwhelm NATO and everything in its path, notwithstanding the constant fear of the use of nuclear, biological and chemical weapons on the battlefield - and therefore in the populated heartland of Europe.

Despite the qualitative superiority of Western equipment in general, the sheer numerical superiority of Warsaw Pact over NATO forces in virtually every category of troops and equipment had become so marked that the prevailing defensive doctrine - which envisaged NATO forces withdrawing in good order while inflicting an unacceptable level of attrition on the enemy - was becoming increasingly delusional. Western defence planners were faced with the unattractive fact that their only realistic recourse in the face of the unleashing of the Soviet juggernaut would be the early use of tactical nuclear weapons, with the inevitable consequence of (probably rapid) escalation to a full exchange of thermonuclear devices.

It was proposed that the British Army and its NATO allies should adopt a more flexible response whereby highly mobile all-arms battle groups would manoeuvre rapidly to engage the enemy at the decisive point, to inflict the maximum damage and impediment to any offensive. Fundamental to this concept was new and more capable equipment such as Warrior. For many years the FV432 had been employed as a 'battlefield taxi', to transport troops close to the point of action; on arrival the infantry would disembark to conduct offensive or defensive tactical operations of a type which would be essentially familiar to any veteran of World War II. The new doctrine saw Warrior and Challenger moving in intimate mutual support, supported by the concentrated firepower of highly co-ordinated artillery and close attack aircraft. The infantry were now to arrive practically on the objective before 'debussing' for the final assault, while the newly vacated Warriors moved to predetermined positions to add their own volume of firepower to the proceedings. Once the position had been neutralised, the infantry would clamber aboard their Warriors and proceed to the next target.

These tactics were used in earnest by the British Army for the first time during the Gulf War of 1991, and with devastating effect. The Warrior/Challenger battle groups of 4th and 7th Armoured Brigades, 1st (UK) Armoured Division proved to be highly successful against Iraqi opposition. The 7th Armoured Brigade was 'tank heavy', the Warriors of 1st Bn, The Staffordshire Regiment (The Prince of Wales's) fighting alongside the Challengers of the Royal Scots Dragoon Guards and the Queen's Royal Irish Hussars. The 4th Brigade was 'infantry heavy', with Warriors of 1st Bn, The Royal Scots (The Royal Regiment) and 3rd Bn, The Royal Fusiliers serving alongside Challengers of the 14th/20th King's Hussars.

Within 18 months, Warrior was on a completely different field of conflict and fulfilling a completely different and more complex mission. In 1991-92 the former Republic of Yugoslavia disintegrated in turmoil, its long-suppressed internecine hatreds flaring up in a chaotic series of armed conflicts darkened by mutual atrocities against civilian populations. An appalled world reacted; in February-June 1992 United Nations contingents (UNPROFOR) were deployed to Bosnia in an attempt to stabilise the situation and to monitor various short-lived local ceasefires. Britain's initial UN contingent included the Warrior-mounted 1st Bn, The Cheshire Regiment, which took responsibility for escorting humanitarian aid convoys through a large western sector of that devastated land. This was a mission of some delicacy, given the chaotic communal divisions within their sector, and UNPROFOR's very restricted mandate; it demanded courage, determination and cool judgement of all ranks of the battalions which served successively in Bosnia over the years which followed.

Temporarily war-weary but unreconciled, the Serbian, Croatian and Bosnian Muslim combatants grudgingly agreed to the US-sponsored Dayton peace accords in December 1995. Made wary by experience, the UN Security Council transferred authority to an International Peace Implementation Force (IFOR), under NATO command and with a much more robustly defined mission. Over the past three years Warrior units have continued to rotate through IFOR's Multi-National Division South-West.

* * *

Wherever it is to be employed, Warrior remains a potent weapon system which enjoys the confidence of its crews - who refer to their armoured home and instrument of war simply as 'the wagon'. When soldiers take their equipment for granted with this kind of casual familiarity, no other accolade is necessary.

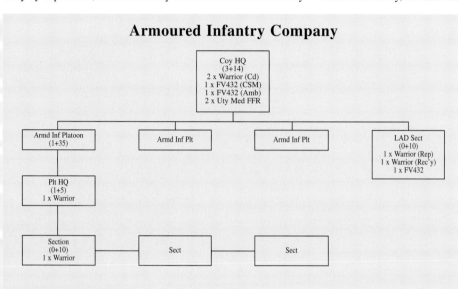

Armoured Infantry Company

```
                          ┌──────────────────┐
                          │     Coy HQ       │
                          │     (3+14)       │
                          │  2 x Warrior (Cd)│
                          │  1 x FV432 (CSM) │
                          │  1 x FV432 (Amb) │
                          │  2 x Uty Med FFR │
                          └──────────────────┘
        ┌──────────────────┬────────┴─────────┬──────────────────┐
┌───────────────┐  ┌───────────────┐  ┌───────────────┐  ┌────────────────┐
│Armd Inf Platoon│ │  Armd Inf Plt │  │  Armd Inf Plt │  │   LAD Sect     │
│    (1+35)     │  └───────────────┘  └───────────────┘  │    (0+10)      │
└───────────────┘                                         │1 x Warrior (Rep)│
        │                                                 │1 x Warrior (Rec'y)│
┌───────────────┐                                         │  1 x FV432     │
│    Plt HQ     │                                         └────────────────┘
│    (1+5)      │
│  1 x Warrior  │
└───────────────┘
        │
┌───────────────┬──────────────────┬──────────────────┐
│   Section     │  ┌───────────────┐  ┌───────────────┐
│    (0+10)     │  │     Sect      │  │     Sect      │
│  1 x Warrior  │  └───────────────┘  └───────────────┘
└───────────────┘
```

(**Below**) A pre-production prototype of a Warrior Section Vehicle awaits delivery; ten were built at the GKN works at Cable Street, Wolverhampton, between 1980 and 1984. Production began at a new purpose-built factory at Telford, Shropshire, in January 1986, involving 207 component suppliers; principal sub-contracters were Vickers Defence Systems for the complete turret, together with the 30mm Rarden cannon from Royal Ordnance Nottingham, and Perkins Engines (Shrewsbury) for the powerpack. The main components of the Warrior Section Vehicle by percentage of value are turret 33%; powerpack 23%; sights 7%; dampers 5%; track 3%; final drive and roadwheels 3%, and NBC pack 2%. (GKN Defence)

(**Right**) The first 290 production Warriors were handed over to the British Army in May 1987, of which 170 were section vehicles and the remainder specialised variants. The first unit to be equipped with Warrior was 1st Bn, Grenadier Guards, which was declared operational in the armoured infantry role in mid-1988.

In 1993, after the collapse of the Soviet Union, the order for 1,048 was reduced to 789 of which 387 are section vehicles and 105 are for the transport of Anti-Tank Guided Weapon teams - currently equipped with Milan, but eventually with Trigat, a new tri-national medium range missile. (GKN Defence)

(**Left**) One of the most important variants of Warrior is the Mechanised Combat Repair Vehicle, of which 103 have been procured as the FV512. With its callsign Two Four Bravo, this MCRV manned by members of the Royal Electrical and Mechanical Engineers (REME) is attached to B Squadron of The Royal Scots Dragoon Guards during an exercise on Salisbury Plain. Warrior repair and recovery variants serve in both tank and armoured infantry units. The repair variants have the same Perkins powerpack as the section vehicle plus a 3-cylinder diesel Auxiliary Power Unit for operating the crane and the air-compressor for the on-board power tools; an electro-hydraulic pump even allows the MCRV to change its own powerpack. (Simon Dunstan)

(**Right**) The most sophisticated variant of the Warrior family is the Mechanised Artillery Observation Vehicle, as used by Forward Observation Officers with Royal Artillery field regiments. With its four radio antennae it is similar in configuration to the standard command variant; but the MAOV has a dummy main gun, to free up the internal space required by the communications and fire control equipment carried. The MAOV, of which the Army operates 52, was rushed into service ahead of schedule during the Gulf War, which required timely and comprehensive training support from GKN and its sub-contractors Pilkington, Dowty and GEC to assist the Army in commissioning the new vehicles and to provide qaulified instructors and REME personnel to teach the troops in the field. (GKN Defence)

(**Left**) A less complex version of MAOV is the Battery Command Vehicle; 19 are in service, one per battery in each RA field regiment. Again, it has a dummy gun and four radio antennae; a further identification feature of these and command vehicles are additional stowage boxes on the turret sides (although many infantry crews have also acquired these for their section vehicles). The BCV has two VRC 353 radios; the MOAV has two 353s and two 351s.

Warrior is constructed of an aluminium hull and a steel turret providing armour protection against 14.5mm AP rounds, shell fragments from 155mm air bursts and anti-tank mines up to 9kg. (Simon Dunstan)

7

(Above) One of the fundamental requirements was for Warrior to be able to accompany Challenger MBTs into battle. Here, Warriors of 2 Plt, No.1 Coy, 1st Bn, Coldstream Guards conduct an assault in conjunction with a Challenger 1 of A Sqn The King's Royal Hussars on the Bergen-Hohne training area. The door central in the hull side covers the NBC filtration system. Eight armoured infantry battalions are equipped with Warrior: six stationed in Germany - two each in 4th, 7th and 20th Armd Bdes; and two in the UK - one each in 1st and 19th Mech Brigades. Others are used by the Combined Arms Training Centre at Warminster and BATUS in Canada. (Simon Dunstan)

(Right) Officer students on a company commanders' course plan for the next serial during Exercise Phantom Bugle - the largest armoured exercise conducted in UK, which happens three times a year. These soldiers are wearing the recently introduced 95 Pattern combat clothing. These Warriors of the CATC armoured infantry battalion are the busiest in the British Army, with an average track mileage of 5,000 miles (8,000km) - the mileage allocated to this one unit is almost half that of the whole of 1 (UK) Armoured Division in Germany.

(Opposite top) The view from a Warrior turret during an FTX (Field Training Exercise) on Salisbury Plain. The vehicle commander normally sits in the right hand position where he also acts as loader for the 30mm Rarden, which is laid and fired by the gunner to his left; in this photo the left hand seat is occupied by a Royal Tank Regiment major (note black coverall with white tank arm badge). Note the map attached to the back of the sight in front of him; this is virtually standard operating procedure for Warrior turret crews, as is the taping of a piece of acetate to the sight to displaying the callsign matrix - keeping a chinograph handy allows them to jot down changes in BATCO or radio frequencies as required. (Simon Dunstan)

(Left) Named after the Peninsular War battle honour CIUDAD RODRIGO, an FV511 command vehicle of C Coy, 1st Bn, The Worcestershire and Sherwood Foresters Regiment advances to contact during an exercise on Salisbury Plain; the callsign Zero Bravo on the turret stowage box denotes the company commander. The companies are indicated by the traditional outlines – a triangle, a square and a circle respectively.

The "Woofers", as they are commonly known, bear the lineage of the old 29th, 36th, 45th and 95th Regiments of Foot. As the cost of training battalions in the armoured infantry role is so high, it is customary for them to undertake a tour of duty of up to six years rather than the two years of a standard infantry posting. (Simon Dunstan)

A fire team disembark from their section vehicle during a TESEX on Salisbury Plain while a Challenger 1 Mark 2 provides covering fire; these AFVs are finished in the yellow and green camouflage of OPFOR (Opposing Forces), and fitted with Direct Fire Weapons Effect Simulators. DFWES produce the sound of weapons firing (hence the loudspeakers above the smoke dischargers), while a laser firing device replicates the capabilities of the main armament against various targets - be they personnel or AFVs - all of which carry receptors to assess the notional damage inflicted.

(Above) The companion vehicle to MCRV is the Mechanised Recovery Vehicle (Repair); a Warrior company has one of each. While both have a 6.5 tonne telescopic crane with a maximum reach of 4.52 metres capable of lifting a complete Challenger 1 or 2 MBT powerpack, the MRV(R) is also fitted with a twin capstan winch of 20 tonnes capacity, and a rear-mounted earth anchor to provide stability during recovery operations. The yellow device beside the stowed crane is an engine lifting beam. This vehicle also has a driver's windscreen complete with perspex sidescreens, which is unusual in the UK - it tends to get in the way - though a welcome protection against wind chill during a Bosnian winter. (Simon Dunstan)

(Opposite top) With one of its many stowage bins open, an FV512 MCRV of 2nd Bn, The Royal Anglian Regiment is prepared for action prior to a battle group exercise on Salisbury Plain. Across the hull front are A-frame towing bars, and above them are kinetic energy towing ropes with connecting shackles attached to speed recovery of stranded vehicles. Warrior repair vehicles are fitted with a one-man turret mounting the same 7.62mm chain gun as the co-axial armament of the standard section vehicle. The MCRV is well equipped with tools and spare parts to allow many repairs to be undertaken in the field. (Simon Dunstan)

(Right) Warrior section vehicle of 2nd Royal Anglians undergoing brake testing at the CATC, Warminster, before taking part in an exercise on Salisbury Plain. Warrior's brakes are so efficient that it can stop within its own length; this has been the cause of several road accidents in Germany when vehicles that have been travelling too close behind

have impacted under a Warrior and then been crushed as it settles back on its suspension. Warning signs are now carried on all Warriors travelling on German roads. Note that the rear mudflaps hang down fully when driving on roads but are folded up for cross-country running. When folded up they stop mud from compacting under the trackguards, as well as obliterating the rear lights. When down they minimise the dust plume being thrown up to the inconvenience of other vehicles; and reduce the chances of track pads - which sometimes come loose during road travel - flying up to hit following vehicles. (However, it is not uncommon for German drivers to purloin discarded track pads and keep them in their cars until such time as their vehicles suffer body damage, when they produce the track pad and claim compensation from the British Army.) (Simon Dunstan)

(Above & opposite top) A comparison between the two repair and recovery variants shows the principal differences, the most notable being the rear-mounted earth anchor of the FV513 Mechanised Recovery Vehicle (Repair) or MRV(R). The FV512 Mechanised Combat Vehicle (Repair) or MCRV has a hydraulic stabiliser at the left rear corner to provide stability during lifting operations. These two REME vehicles are attached to 1st Bn The Worcestershire and Sherwood Foresters Regiment of 1st (Mechanised) Brigade during Exercise First Crusade on Salisbury Plain. (Simon Dunstan)

(Right) In an ecstasy of fumbling, a Warrior commander dons his S10 respirator as the company comes under simulated gas attack. Note the mudflaps hooked up for cross-country running, and the rear light clusters covered with hessian to keep them clean and eliminate tell-tale reflections. This measure is also useful at night, to reduce the intensity of the lights to a level which allows following vehicles to see them but does not show up the Warrior at any distance. This FV510 section vehicle has a single large power-operated rear door; command vehicles and artillery variants have a double split door which is opened manually.(Simon Dunstan)

(**Opposite top**) A Warrior section vehicle carries a crew of three and seven riflemen in the troop compartment, with four down the right hand side and three opposite them; this photograph is taken looking backwards from the forward right hand position beside the turret basket - the normal position for the most junior member of the section. The soldier in the right foreground is seated on (though not, we hasten to add, using) the chemical toilet, which is only used under NBC conditions - it is normally employed for extra stowage. The section leader is seated beside the door with the button to open the hydraulically operated door above his head; he also has a vision block to give him some indication of the situation outside, although it is up to the turret crew to keep him informed. Obscured here on the floor between the two nearest soldiers is the essential BV or boiling vessel, which is frequently in use on exercise to provide a constant flow of tea and heated rations - it is also the only source of heating in the troop compartment. These soldiers are from Burma Coy, 1st Bn, The King's Own Royal Border Regiment. (Simon Dunstan)

(**Left**) A Warrior commander receives his orders as he checks the track tension with a socket spanner, while the driver (left) tightens the track by pumping grease into the hydraulic mounting arm of the rear idler. It is apparent why Warrior crews prefer to operate their vehicles without trackguards fitted - it makes track and suspension maintenance much simpler. Although Warrior has proved to be admirably reliable in service this is only achieved through constant and thorough maintenance procedures. Note the camouflage netting stowage basket along the top of the hull side. (Simon Dunstan)

(**Above**) Members of a rifle section relax in the back of their wagon during an FTX on Salisbury Plain. Even with only four men in the troop compartment space is at a premium, with their personal kit stowed behind the nylon web netting. Although each crew position has seatbelts to restrain the occupant in case of accident - mandatory because of health and safety regulations - these are in fact impossible to wear when in full Combat Equipment Fighting Order.

Note that the turret cage has been covered with black gaffer tape to reduce dust and draught entering the troop compartment. Below the turret cage is the fuel tank; since this is made of translucent polyethelene the diesel fuel is visible as it slops about. This has a mesmerising effect and can induce motion sickness - a disconcerting experience for a new recruit, since there is nowhere to be sick (as his comrades will quickly point out) except into his own helmet. He then has to cradle this in his lap until the vehicle halts at the next objective, where he debusses and has to empty his helmet of vomit before putting it on his head to continue the assault. (Simon Dunstan)

BATUS

For 25 years all-arms battle groups have trained on the 2,500 square kilometres of rolling prairie in Alberta, Canada, known as BATUS (British Army Training Unit Suffield). Exercise Medicine Man is a deployment held six times a year between spring and autumn; each gives a battle group some of the most realistic training possible, with live firing of all types of weapons including MBT main armament and AS90 self-propelled howitzers. This often causes grass fires in the parched summer months.

(Above) A Warrior section vehicle halts during an exercise. The 'lollypop' on the turret roof is a weapons state indicator (WSI) - white shows that all weapons are clear of ammunition and uncocked.

(Left) At BATUS almost all Warriors have trackguards fitted to reduce the amount of dust blown up, whereas in Europe they are usually omitted to ease track maintenance. The yellow - over-green BATUS camouflage is similar to that used by OPFOR Warriors in the UK.

(Above) Two Warriors of 1st Coy advance to contact. The red weapons state indicator, denoting that weapons are ready to fire, is welded to the shutter of the gunner's primary sight. With the shutter closed as here, it denotes that live ammunition is loaded but the safety catch is engaged; it becomes vertical when the shutter is opened, showing that the Warrior is ready to fire either the 30mm main armament or the co-axial 7.62mm chain gun. The red square on the hull side is a flexible flap covering a fire extinguisher pull handle which activates fire suppressant agents in the engine compartment.

(Right) A pair of section vehicles rest in dead ground. The white stripes on the gun mantlet - 'forty-fives' - are a safety feature to ensure that the main armament is only fired under prescribed conditions. This crew have avoided safety regulations by covering the red WSI with a sandbag so that the gunner can still use his primary sight.

(Opposite top) An infantryman deploys a 94mm Light Anti-Tank Weapon (LAW), with his Warrior section vehicle in the background. This is one of 13 weapons systems in an armoured infantry company, which is indicative of the weight of firepower available to a force commander on the modern battlefield. Note the white weapons state indicator meaning all guns are clear; and the white bands painted on the radio antennae, which make them less visible against the sky. The white-painted surround to the callsign One Two indicates a Warrior of 2nd Coy at BATUS.

(Left) The configuration of radio antennae indicates that this Warrior is a command variant; but the lack of its main armament shows that the dummy gun has been lost, so this is a Mechanised Artillery Observation Vehicle as used by Royal Artillery FOOs

(Forward Observation Officers). At BATUS each 'Med Man' exercise comprises approximately 1,200 men and 400 vehicles including 120 AFVs, of which 42 are Warriors. The Warrior MAOV advances with the infantry section vehicles to control the fire of the battle group's six AS90 155mm self-propelled howitzers, which are capable of delivering 18 rounds in ten seconds as fire support. Note the exhaust shroud of the auxiliary power unit on the hull side; an APU is fitted to Royal Artillery variants and those of the Royal Electrical and Mechanical Engineers to provide increased electrical power for the extra communications equipment or power tools and cranes.

BATUS allows realistic training of all the complex elements of modern armoured warfare on a scale impossible in heavily populated Europe. On the empty prairie the force

commander can co-ordinate all the elements within the battle group - MBTs, Warriors, armoured engineers, self-propelled artillery - with support from air assets plus any other heavy weapons held by higher formations. The treeless but rolling terrain is also excellent for teaching a keen appreciation of the skills of concealed movement.

(Above) Infantrymen catch some sleep beside their section vehicle during an exercise at BATUS. Each 'Med Man' comprises various serials of section and company training before a 72-hour battle group live firing exercise, culminating in a seven-day TESEX using DFWES. If activated by an OPFOR laser, the computer system will assess the coded information to determine if the attacker's weapon is of sufficient effect to destroy the target or to inflict a mobility kill,

whereby the engine is automatically shut down. Although expensive, DFWES has radically altered the conduct and outcome of many FTXs, particularly at BATUS where OPFOR Scorpions and Spartans are configured by the computer system to act as T-80s and BMPs.

In all, 23 days are spent on the prairie during a 'Med Man', and sleep is a luxury. It is SOP for all Warrior personnel to sleep down one side of the vehicle, here down the right hand side, where the engine compartment gives off residual heat at night. It also produces the clearest indication to other vehicles using thermal imaging to manoeuvre during the hours of darkness, so that they know not to pass too close to the Warrior for fear of crushing men on the ground.

DPTA

With the collapse of the Soviet Union and the Warsaw Pact new training areas have become available in the countries of former adversaries including the Czech Republic, Hungary and Poland. The latter has provided a large training area at Drawsko-Pomorskie in Pomerania, 80 miles east of the Polish/German border. The first battle group FTX, Exercise Uhlan Eagle, was held there in September 1996.

(Below) The turret crew of an MAOV of 40th Regiment Royal Artillery scan the heavily wooded battlefield during Exercise Uhlan Eagle. The headlights are covered with hessian to avoid reflections from the glass. Draped across the front of the Warrior is an inter-vehicle starting cable, and tow ropes are attached to the lifting hooks for rapid recovery - which, in DPTA, is more often than not due to driving into swampy ground rather than to breakdown, since Warrior is a highly reliable AFV.

(Right) Warriors of 1st Bn, The Royal Highland Fusiliers (1RHF) are prepared at the outset of the first exercise in the Drawsko - Pomorksie Training Area (DPTA).

(Right) 'Train Green' has been a tenet of the British Army for many years particularly in Germany and the UK, where covering vehicles with local vegetation is no longer allowed, in the name of ecological correctness. The closure of many training areas has obliged the Army to find new venues for FTXs, such as DPTA, where more realistic training is permitted in the skills fundamental to survival in time of war. Here, Warriors of 7 Plt, C Coy, 1RHF - suitably bedecked, but with optics and callsigns unobscured - move forward with Challengers of 2RTR bringing up the rear.

(**Left**) With the national flags of the UK and Poland streaming from the front two radio antennae of his Warrior command vehicle, the regimental banner of the Royal Highland Fusiliers flies aloft as the Warrior of the commanding officer of 1RHF, Lt Col W.Loudon MBE, returns to dry land after negotiating a pontoon bridge constructed by the Polish 3rd (Roads & Bridges) Engineer Regt at the outset of Exercise Uhlan Eagle, September 1996. National and 'tribal' flags were a feature of the first battle group exercise in Poland; but none could match the size of the CO 2 Royal Tank Regiment, which provided the 7th Armoured Brigade tank element of Uhlan Eagle 96.

24

(**Opposite top**) The DPTA is heavily forested and has numerous rivers and lakes, providing a complete contrast to BATUS and requiring extensive Royal Engineer support. Here, a section vehicle of 1RHF plunges into a river; Warrior has a fording depth of 1.3 metres. Note that the armoured shutter for the commander's sight is closed while the gunner's is open, showing the Raven combined day/night sight.

(**Left**) Callsign Zero Bravo identifies the commander of No.3 Coy, 1st Bn, Coldstream Guards during Exercise Prairie Eagle, April 1997. Note the laser designator of the DFWES above the cannon, and receptors above the smoke dischargers and on the turret basket. The Army has 84 command vehicles in service: while the section vehicle has one VRC 353 and two 349 radios fitted, the FV511 has two 353 and one 351, and the FV510 of platoon headquarters has two 350, one 351 and one 353.

(**Above**) Warrior of A Coy, 2nd Bn, Royal Regiment of Fusiliers and a REME MRV(R) crossing the Zly Leg river on a PP64 ferry manned by men of the Polish 1st Eng Bde during Uhlan Eagle. The tubing over the section vehicle's Rarden is to simulate a BMP variant - 2 RRF were acting as "enemy".

Active service: The Gulf, 1990-91

(Below) After hectic weeks of preparation in Germany, the Warriors of 1st Bn, The Staffordshire Regiment - the armoured infantry element of 7th Armoured Brigade Group - were landed at the port of Al Jubayl in Saudi Arabia during the last week of October 1990. In its newly-applied coat of sand yellow, a Warrior section vehicle stands on the quayside awaiting automotive modifications to enhance reliability in the sandy and dusty conditions of the Middle East. This Warrior has an inter-vehicle starting cable across the hull front, to assist any other whose batteries had become discharged during the long sea voyage despite the best efforts of the maintenance teams that accompanied the Warriors on board the Ro-Ro ferry from Germany. (Kevin Gifford)

(Right) Towing a GKN Defence T4 high mobility trailer carrying spare parts, an FV512 Mechanised Combat Repair Vehicle moves off after assisting B Sqn, Royal Scots Dragoon Guards in their Challenger 1 Mark 3 MBTs. Note the Challenger fanbelts looped over the driver's rear view mirror; and again, the anti-reflection hessian over the headlight clusters.

(Below right) Once deployed into the desert the Staffords began intensive training, starting with sections, then in companies, then as a complete battalion, before battle group and brigade exercises with the Challengers of Royal Scots Dragoon Guards and Queen's Royal Irish Hussars. This took place firstly at Al Fadili and the Jerboa range for gunnery, and then on Devil Dog Dragoon range, which the Desert Rats shared with the US Marines under whose command they initially came.

This section vehicle taking part in one of the early exercises bears the callsign indicating the Battle Captain of B Sqn, Scots DG. The vehicle has rolls of CARM (Chemical Agent Resistant Material) along the trackguards and hull front to mask the suspension and tracks when halted.

(Above) A REME Mechanised Combat Repair Vehicle, callsign Two Four Bravo, deploys its telescopic crane to lift the engine decks of a Challenger 1 Mark 3 of B Sqn, Scots DG. Note the leg of the stabiliser extended into the sand; together with a suspension lock-out system this provides the necessary stability to lift the weight of a Challenger powerpack. This MCRV has had a ladder added at the rear for easy access to the Chieftain stowage bins fitted on the roof. When fully laden in the repair role, the vehicle weighs 28.5 tonnes with a maximum speed of 70km/h to a maximum range of 500km.

(Opposite top) One of the most important modifications made to Warrior during Operation Granby was the design and development of an appliqué Chobham armour kit, which was fitted to all section vehicles and RA variants prior to the ground offensive. Here, an FV513 Mechanised Recovery Vehicle (Repair) assists in the fitting of Chobham armour panels to the Warrior of the second-in-command of Support Coy, 1st Staffords. It was calculated that it would take about 12 hours to fit the complete package, but with practice vehicles were being fitted out within four hours. In the words of one REME fitter, 'It wasn't technically difficult, it was just like reading a big Airfix model plan.' Note that when Chobham armour is fitted to Warrior it is not possible to tow the vehicle from the front using the exisiting towing pintles.

(Right) Warrior section vehicle displaying its recently fitted Chobham armour, the panels down the sides incorporating brackets for water jerrycans; the driver is protected by an armour slab complete with a POL hopper to carry drums of engine oil and transmission fluid. No armour was fitted to the engine compartment for fear of compromising cooling of the powerpack. Although designed primarily to thwart attack by infantry anti-tank weapons, the armour more than proved its worth during the ground offensive when, in an unfortunate incident of 'friendly fire', a Warrior of 1st Staffords was hit in the side by a HESH round fired by a Challenger. This caused the Chobham armour panel to disintegrate, but only dented the actual hull; the occupants were dazed but unhurt, although an officer who had been standing nearby was seriously wounded in the legs. Despite damage to the electrical and communications systems, the Warrior continued with the battle group until the end of the war.

(Left) To bring the armoured infantry battalions up to wartime strength they were reinforced with men wearing many cap badges. Understandably, those on attachment wished to retain their identity and operate as complete entities; e.g., 1st Staffords had a section in its Milan Platoon composed of Royal Greenjackets, while 3 RRF had many Queen's Own Highlanders in its ranks. As the original battalion to be equipped with Warrior 1st Bn, Grenadier Guards was much in demand to reinforce both brigades, particularly for its very experienced drivers. Accordingly, many Guardsmen were dispersed throughout the units in the Gulf. Although The Queen's Company as a whole was attached to The Royal Scots, it fought during the offensive in the 14th/20th Hussars Battle Group; and No.2 Company was attached to 3 RRF. These two Warrior section vehicles can be identified as manned by Guardsmen by the pennants in the blue/red/blue of The Household Division.

On 22 November 1990 it was announced that 4th Armoured Brigade would be sent to the Gulf to combine with 7th Armoured Brigade Group to form 1st (UK) Armoured Division. 4th Armoured Brigade comprised 1st Bn, The Royal Scots (The Royal Regiment); 3rd Bn, The Royal Regiment of Fusiliers; and 14th/20th King's Hussars reinforced by A Sqn, The Life Guards. In total there were more than 300 Warriors in theatre during Operation Granby. Most of the training assets were then devoted to 4th Armd Bde, which had a stiff learning curve to overcome as the date of the ground offensive loomed. Unfortunately the brigade was to suffer the highest British casualties of the war when two Warrior section vehicles were hit by Maverick guided missiles fired from a USAF A-10 Thunderbolt II close air support aircraft.

Final preparations are made to the section vehicles of C Coy, 1st Staffords in the last hours before the land offensive - codenamed Operation Desert Sabre by the British. The black chevron, designed as a mutual identification sign within the Coalition forces, was one of the last markings to be applied. Note that headlight, sidelight and traffic indicator lenses have been painted over leaving only narrow slits to provide illumination. The POL hopper on the leading vehicle is filled with boxes of combat rations. Improvised towing cables have been attached to the lifting eyes leading to a single large shackle, to speed recovery - the standard towing pintle is covered by the supplementary Chobham armour. As a rule of thumb, Warrior crews dispensed with any item which was not readily used within a three-day period; e.g., seat belts, floor plates, spare sights, etc. were discarded and buried if they could not be disposed of to rear echelon vehicles - removal of the floor plates made room for extra ammunition boxes.

(**Opposite top**) A TOW Lynx anti-tank helicopter of 4th Regt, Army Air Corps swoops low over the Tactical HQ of the Staffords Battle Group; Lt Col Charles Rogers, the commanding officer, stands in characteristic posture behind his Warrior FV511 command vehicle, callsign One One Bravo (on the rear and turret sides). Just visible here as a black mark ahead of the turret callsign is the battalion insignia of the Staffordshire knot superimposed on a palm tree, recalling the World War II insignia of the Afrika Korps. Above the chevron on the hull side is the vehicle name - FEROZESHAH, the regiment's greatest battle honour, gained in 1845 during the First Sikh War. The other vehicles in the Tac HQ are CVR(T) Spartans of 1 Field Sqn, 21 Engineer Regt, and in the background FV432 armoured ambulances.

(**Opposite bottom**) During the week leading up to the ground offensive British and US artillery bombarded the Iraqi positions opposite the US VII Corps lines with the equivalent explosive power of 75,000 Scud missiles - of which the Iraqis fired 81 throughout the war. With the red jerboa of 7th Armoured Brigade on the forward Chobham armour panel, the MAOV of Lt Col Rory Clayton, commanding officer of 40th Field Regt RA, accompanies the Tactical HQ of Brig Patrick Cordingley in the advance to provide rapid artillery support. The weight of firepower of the gun and MLRS (Multiple Launch Rocket System) batteries controlled from this one vehicle during Operation Desert Sabre was greater than that available to Gen Montgomery during the battle of El Alamein in 1942. Note the orange air recognition panel above the turret stowage basket; and the crew's Bergens covered in CARM on the hull sides.

(**Above**) Warrior of 1st Bn, Royal Scots standing by as Iraqi prisoners are fed and watered following their capture. It has a small St Andrew's cross marked on the turret; and its callsign indicates the battalion Intelligence Officer, whose responsibilites include the identification and interrogation of POWs. As part of 4th Armoured Brigade, the Royal Scots Battle Group swept through the various enemy brigade-sized objectives which were codenamed after metals - Bronze, Brass and Tungsten. Within 100 hours the Iraqi army was broken. Throughout the ground war Warrior availability exceeded 95 per cent, with two vehicles being destroyed and one damaged - all due to 'friendly fire'. To the rifleman in the smelly, sweaty and claustrophobic troop compartment, Warrior had been his home for many months and, for almost all, had carried him into battle and to a famous victory.

Active service: Bosnia since 1992

(Below) In the white United Nations livery of peacekeeping forces, an immaculately painted Warrior of 5 Plt, 1st Bn, The Cheshire Regiment disembarks from the Ro-Ro (roll on, roll off) ferry *Rosa Dan* at the port of Split on 11 November 1992 in support of United Nations Protection Force 2 (UNPROFOR 2) in the former Republic of Yugoslavia. Many of the Cheshires' Warriors had served with the Staffords during the Gulf War; in the space of 18 months they had gone from green to sand, back to green, and then to white - a reflection on the wide commitments and adaptability of the British Army of the 1990s.

(Right) Flying regimental pennants of cerise red over buff, marked with the white 22 of their old number in the Line, Warriors of 1 Cheshire Battle Group pause on a track during the journey from Tomislavgrad to Vitez at the outset of Operation Grapple. As the column negotiated the Dynaric Alps in central Bosnia the temperature plummeted and, amid swirling blizzards, the narrow roads turned into ice rinks upon which some Warriors skidded and spun uncontrollably. More than one vehicle slipped off the roads, causing serious recovery problems for the REME mechanics, whose expertise has reached new heights during deployments to former Yugoslavia. Note that the MRV(R) in the foreground flies the REME colours of blue, yellow and red below the Cheshire pennant.

(Below right) Soon after its arrival in Vitez the 1 Cheshire Battle Group conducted an operation to find a route to Tuzla that was suitable for Warriors and UNHCR trucks carrying much-needed humanitarian aid. Here Lt Col Bob Stewart, the commanding officer of the Cheshires, moves off in his FV511 command vehicle with the Warriors and an FV432 of A Coy during this three-day operation. Note the transponder stalk of the GPS (Global Positioning System) on his 'Five Eleven', which was christened JULIET. For his outstanding leadership during Operation Grapple Lt Col Stewart was awarded the Distinguished Service Order; his battalion set the standard by which those that followed would be judged.

(**Opposite top**) The 1 Cheshire Battle Group at the outset of Operation Grapple comprised 46 Warriors and 34 Scimitars; eight of the latter were in the Reconnaissance Platoon, the remainder being manned by B Sqn, 9th/12th Royal Lancers. The Cheshires themselves were reinforced by 100 soldiers of 2nd Bn, The Royal Irish Regiment. The fundamental role of the battle group was to escort humanitarian aid convoys of the UN High Commission for Refugees (UNHCR) to any community which needed them throughout the war-devastated country, irrespective of nationality or religion. Here, Warriors of 1 Plt pause on a road with, in the foreground, an MCRV towing a 6.5 tonne High Mobility Maintenance Support Trailer. Capable of being towed at high cross-country speeds by Warrior repair variants, the GKN Defence T4 trailer is equipped with a system of quick-release

mounting points enabling it to carry either one Challenger powerpack or two smaller ones such as Warrior, FV432 or Chieftain engines. (GKN Defence)

(**Left**) Some of the items that form the standard kit of a Warrior are laid out for an inventory check behind Zero Charlie, the command vehicle of the second-in-command of C Coy, 1st Cheshires, Capt Nick Fenton; note the twin split rear doors of the command variant. In a Warrior section vehicle this amount of kit has to be stowed inside together with 219 rounds of 30mm and 2,200 rounds of 7.62mm ammunition for the turret guns; LAW 94 anti-tank missiles; 51mm mortar with ammunition; combat rations; and, last but not least, ten men with their personal kit in Bergen rucksacks and their SA80 rifles, each with at least 120 rounds of 5.56mm ammunition.

(**Above**) In the last few months of the Cheshires' deployment the situation in central Bosnia deteriorated markedly, with vicious fighting between Croats and Muslims and many barbaric atrocities committed in the course of 'ethnic cleansing'. In May 1993 a major roulement of British troops occurred; the Cheshires were replaced by 1st Bn, The Prince of Wales's Own Regiment of Yorkshire (more easily known as the 'Yorkies') on a six-month tour as part of Operation Grapple 2. The battalion's major role

remained the escort of humanitarian aid throughout its area.

Here, Sgt Sadler's section vehicle of 2 Plt, 1 PWO on patrol flies a UN flag - national flags had been deemed inappropriate on a UN operation. Note the addition of the towing pintle on the hull front Chobham armour panel, one of the first modifications to be made in Bosnia; it simplifies recovery on narrow Bosnian roads, allowing the Warrior to be towed from the front once more.

(Above) Sgt Cunningham and his crew from 7 Plt pause during a convoy escort operation; the two riflemen in the rear troop compartment provide 'top cover' following standard Northern Ireland practice. Note the 'rocking horse' insignia (the White Horse of Hanover) from the 1 PWO cap badge faintly visible below the Union Flag on the turret side; and the prominent bolt heads securing the Chobham armour panels to the hull sides. Prudent crews always check and tighten these bolts regularly; failure to do so after extensive road running can cause them to come loose, resulting in a panel falling off. As Chobham armour remains secret the loss of a panel would constitute a dire misdemeanour to be avoided at all costs. Similarly, should a panel be damaged in a road traffic accident it must be covered immediately with tape or tarpaulin against prying eyes.

(Opposite top) Road accidents remain the single greatest cause of casualties to all the UN forces in former Yugoslavia. Here, a Spartan APC has come to grief and awaits recovery by the Warrior MRV(R) from C Coy, 1 PWO in the background. Despite their age, the Spartans and Scimitars (Combat Vehicle Reconnaissance Tracked, CVRT) - most of which are older than their crews - have proved highly effective in Bosnia, where they are far more capable of negotiating the marginal road system than Warrior. The Spartan has also proved useful for crossing the front lines between the warring factions, on account of its less belligerent appearance, which on many occasions has aided delicate negotiations to allow aid convoys to proceed.

(Right) With its Chobham armour and heavy firepower, Warrior is well protected and capable of neutralising nearly all the weapons deployed by the warring factions. However, mines remain a serious threat; the Yorkies suffered several casualties both in men and machines to mine attacks, including the Warrior of the commanding officer, Lt Col Alastair Duncan. The photograph shows typical damage to a Warrior caused by an anti-tank mine. Although such damage can be readily repaired in theatre, it is usual to return the Warrior to the UK for detailed analysis by defence research scientists so that further measures against mine

attack can be devised and implemented. The majority of anti-tank mines encountered are based on the Soviet TM series but manufactured in former Yugoslavia, with a typical explosive content of 5.6kg. In a 1997 survey of the British-controlled area of Multi-National Division South West alone, it was calculated that there are still 13,292 anti-tank and 50,518 anti-personnel mines to be disposed of. Indeed, it is hazardous to stray onto the verges of roads that have been rendered safe, because the locals deposit there any mines they find for disposal by UN forces.

41

(**Above**) Despite highly skilled drivers there have been many road accidents in Bosnia. For Warrior the major danger is icy winter roads, which turn it into a 30-ton sledge waltzing towards a sheer drop down the mountainside. Fortunately there were no serious casualties when this 1 PWO wagon came to grief, making its crew fully fledged members of the 'Warrior formation flying team'. Any damage caused by the British Army has to be paid for; it is not unknown for a Bosnian mayor to invoice for hundreds of Deutschmarks because Warrior tracks have caused minor damage to kerbstones, in a town which his people and their erstwhile neighbours have already virtually razed to the ground.

(**Right**) 'Track-bashing' remains one of the least enjoyable chores for an AFV crew. Here soldiers of 1 PWO change trackpads, a job which takes a section of ten men almost a whole day. With the amount of road running in Bosnia this must be done every

1,500km, with a complete track change every 4,000km; a typical Warrior drives 6,000km during a six-month tour. As each tracklink costs £113, a track change represents an outlay of almost £18,000. With a good crew a track change can be done in three hours. Road wheels are changed every eight months; the rear idlers are consumed at a more alarming rate, as they take the most punishment in the suspension system.

(**Opposite top**) Through the untiring efforts of the Royal Engineers, many bridges originally built for horses and carts have been strengthened to support 30 tons. This platoon commander's Warrior is equipped with GPS for navigation in difficult terrain, and an additional PRC 320 HF radio to aid communications in broken country; command and platoon leaders' vehicles also have extra power sockets for the laptop computers which are now standard items in an officer's kit.

(Below) Maj Kent-Payne, OC of C Coy, 1 POW renders a recoilless rifle permanently unserviceable under the tracks of his 'Five Eleven'. During their tour as BRITBAT every single UNHCR aid convoy escorted by the Yorkies got through safely, delivering a total of 40,000 tons of aid. These missions often involved protracted negotiations at roadblocks, and the consumption of copious quantities of *slivowitz* (the local plum brandy - to British troops, 'sick-in-the-ditch'). Ten members of the unit were wounded by gunfire, and every single Warrior was hit, the greatest number of impacts in one day being 300. One Warrior was engaged by an M-84 (the Yugoslav version of the T-72 MBT), fortunately without success. When appropriate, the Yorkies' response was vigorous; return fire with the chain guns accounted for 30-40 gunmen during the tour.

44

(Left) A section vehicle of No.2 Coy operating out of Vitez demonstrates its outstanding cross-country agility. In the early years of Operation Grapple many bridges were incapable of bearing the weight of Warrior; patrols and convoy escorts often bypassed the bridges by fording streams and rivers. The UN white colour scheme soon became filthy, and a river was a convenient place to clean them; whenever this happened local children would appear within minutes and volunteer to wash the vehicles in exchange for 'battle bennies' - the boiled sweets from combat ration packs.

(Opposite below) On 12 November 1993 1st Bn, Coldstream Guards assumed the role of BRITBAT 1 from 1 PWO; but even before the handover a Guardsman was injured by Croat snipers in Gornji Vakuf, and on 15 November a major Bosnian Croat offensive shattered a local ceasefire. Here, a Warrior of No.2 Coy picks up speed in the mountain village of Milankovici after passing the notorious 'Bon-Bon Corner', where children congregate to beg for sweets and food as vehicles negotiate several tortuous bends at walking pace. Troops are discouraged from throwing rations to children, however appealing, because of the danger of them falling under the tracks in the ensuing mêlée. Note the driver's use of a windscreen; although it compromises the traverse and depression of the gun, it is highly desirable when travelling at speeds of 40km/h on long winter patrols.

(Below) During the first years of Operation Grapple convoy escort was the fundamental task of the Warrior battalion as part of UNPROFOR. By the time of Grapple 3 the British Army had driven more that 2 ½ million miles on humanitarian aid operations, at a monthly average of 400,000, with each Warrior travelling approximately 1,000km a month. In this classic image, a Warrior of No.3 Coy, 1st Bn, Coldstream Guards and a Scimitar of C Sqn, Light Dragoons bring their 30mm cannons to bear on potential targets during the escort of a UNHCR convoy to Maglaj. Most turret crewmen travel with the hatches upright so that they have armour protection to the rear; some prefer to have them lying flat for better all-round visibility. Note the Guards shoulder flash, and the Bergens in the turret basket - good practice dictates that they should not obscure the rearward vision blocks.

Any external stowage has to be well strapped down or padlocked to the vehicle or in stowage bins to prevent pilfering by the local populace. In Milankovici several aid trucks were stopped and looted by determined crowds of starving women and children despite the heavy-handed attempts of local police or militia to stop them; it is not the policy of UN forces to shoot at unarmed women and children desperate for food.

Although each BRITBAT operated differently according to terrain, season, political situation or numerous other factors, convoy escort was often undertaken by a platoon of Warriors with one or two section vehicles travelling without any 'dismounts' in the rear: if the convoy should come under attack, the drivers of soft-skin vehicles could take cover inside these.

The relentless bombardment of Sarajevo by Bosnian Serb artillery in the surrounding hills continued into 1994, when the arrival of Lt Gen Sir Michael Rose as UNPROFOR commander brought a more robust response. Gen Rose instituted a Heavy Weapon Total Exclusion Zone whereby Serb artillery pieces were to be withdrawn some 20km from the city or be impounded; failure to comply would result in NATO airstrikes. Gen Rose requested a company of his former regiment to supervise the first weapon collection points, and No.2 Coy of the Coldstream was given the task. On leaving the Vitez pocket on 17 February the company commander's Warrior ran over a mine. By a freak of blast effect one roadwheel and damper arm were destroyed but the track remained intact, and the Warrior continued to Sarajevo. On 19 February the company motored through deep snow into the hills around the city - the first British troops to be deployed on Bosnian Serb territory.

(**Opposite top**) A section vehicle of 7 Plt commanded by 2nd Lt 'Zog' Zvegintzov (of White Russian origin, and claiming descent from Genghis Khan …) returns to the company base in the former TV building through the streets of Sarajevo. On the commander's sight cover is the name LEOPARD - No.2 Coy names its vehicles after wild animals, No.1 after regimental battle honours, and No.3 after Royal Navy warships. Note the oil drip tray, emblazoned with '7 Plt 2 Coy', on the engine deck - carrying this tray for use when vehicles are halted is a legal environmental requirement in Germany, but somewhat superfluous in Sarajevo.

(**Left**) Much of the success of Warrior in Bosnia has been due to its powerful psychological effect - whether it be a section vehicle bristling with weapons arriving somewhat incongruously at a local school to rebuild its facilities and then play a soccer match with the locals, or the judicious introduction of a company of Warriors between warring factions to defuse the tension. However, Warrior remains essentially a form of transport for the most important asset of all - the infantryman on the ground. All civil wars are savage; but that in former Yugoslavia has plumbed new depths of barbarity, women and children being butchered with casual indifference by all factions. With their skills and discipline honed in another religious and intercommunal conflict in Northern Ireland, the soldiers of the British Army have brought their particular brand of cool, determined impartiality to this shattered country. L/Sgt Hunter and his section of 3 Plt, No.1 Coy, 1st Bn, Coldstream Guards provide an image representative of them all. The use of Improved Northern Ireland Body Armour (INIBA), with ceramic armour plates to stop high velocity projectiles,

indicates a particularly dangerous area. Although there are 2,700 sets of INIBA in theatre, it is rarely worn instead of standard Combat Body Armour unless there is a specific threat. This photograph shows the typical complement of a Warrior in Bosnia: driver, two men in the turret and four in the back. Manpower commitments rarely allow for more, and four riflemen are adequate for most tasks - as well as giving more space and comfort in the rear compartment.

(**Above**) REME fitters attached to the Coldstream 'pull a powerpack' in a forward company area - a task that takes about 30 minutes with a good crew, and 45 minutes to install a new one. Both the MCRV and MRV(R) have proved invaluable for G-5 operations; their cranes are very useful for repairing and rebuilding the shattered local infrastructure of Bosnia/ Herzegovina.

(Above) L/Cpl Hopkins adopts something approaching the pose of 'The Lincolnshire Poacher', the insignia of 2nd Bn, The Royal Anglian Regiment which adorns the trackguard of this section vehicle of C Coy acting as a checkpoint in Vitez; note also his array of brassard insignia - national flag, battalion title, UN patch, rank chevron, and 7th Armd Bde patch. The 'Poachers' replaced the Coldstream Guards on 8 May 1994 for Operation Grapple 4. Of particular note here is the POL hopper containing two 25-litre drums, one of OMD-80 engine oil and one of WTF (Warrior Transmission Fluid); and the driver's windscreen with its integral wiper. As convoy escort tasks diminished, Warriors were increasingly employed at checkpoints along convoy routes or at points on the confrontation lines. (A contemporary definition by the troops described a checkpoint as 'a 3 million-Deutschmark vehicle and a highly-trained section of the world's finest infantry guarding … er … guarding a sort of road thing'.)

(Opposite) A Warrior of A (Point) Coy, 2nd Royal Anglians undergoes maintenance at the Eko factory at Zepce where the company's echelon was based. The availability rate of Warrior throughout its service in Bosnia/Herzegovina has consistently been over 90 per cent. This is a credit to the REME mechanics, who often work well into the night to ensure that the wagons will be ready for operational duties first thing in the morning; they work on the principle that if there are spares available, any vehicle will be worked on until it is fit for service.

Through successive Grapple deployments, the headquarters of BRITBAT 1 has been in a school at Vitez with a REME Forward Repair Group in a nearby building known as 'The Factory'. Abandoned school buildings have provided convenient billets for Warrior companies, since they usually offer sufficient rooms for the personnel while the tarmac playground acts as a suitable hard standing for the Warriors.

Many troops who have served in the former Yugoslavia remark on the contrast between the beauty of the country and the horror of the atrocities committed by its people. The long-drawn-out agony of Sarajevo was inflicted by Bosnian Serbs who controlled the dominating heights around the city; it was to one such strategic position, Mt Igman, that C Coy of the Poachers were deployed to ensure free passage of humanitarian aid to the city. In temperatures of over 30 degrees C the company found themselves 'on the set of *The Sound of Music*'; and despite being fired on by both Muslims and Serbs, 'acres of white British flesh were roasted in the name of peace'.

(**Right**) A section vehicle of A Coy, 2nd Royal Anglians stands guard at Checkpoint 9 on the confrontation line between the Croats and Muslims at Zavadovici. Note the Poacher emblem on the left trackguard as viewed, and on the right the Sphinx combined with Napoleonic Wars battle honours for Egypt and Talavera - commemorating the battalion's lineage from the old 10th of Foot. Above the gun mantlet is welded a metal stake to cut any wires hung across the roads to decapitate the turret crew.

On 23 February 1994 a peace accord was signed between Bosnian Muslims (BiH) and Croats (HVO) to form the Bosnian Government Federation Forces. With this came an expansion of the area of responsibility of BRITBAT 1 into the 'Maglaj Finger' which, through a quirk of history, contains enclaves of all three warring factions and is thus a microcosm of Bosnia itself. Despite the creation of the confederation a genuine ceasefire proved elusive. In the north is a small Croat enclave around Jelah, whose militia teamed up with the Muslims to fight the Bosnian Serbs (BSA) into whose territory the Maglaj Finger extends. To the south near Zepce the Croats invited the BSA into their area to fight the Muslims in Tersanj, which allowed them - the Croats - to concentrate their forces against the Muslims in Zavadovici. Into this maelstrom of treachery and brutality were committed the Scimitars of D Sqn, Light Dragoons, and the Warriors of the Poachers' A Coy; these had the dubious distinction of being the first British troops to be shelled, mortared and fired upon by all three warring factions.

In one action a Warrior of 3 Plt was engaged by Bosnian Serb small arms, heavy machine guns and direct fire from anti-aircraft guns. In driving rain, the commander returned fire in controlled bursts with his chain gun as he gathered his dismounted troops into his Warrior, and then withdrew in good order down a hazardous mountain track as darkness fell. For his gallantry and coolness under fire, and the measured response befitting UN peacekeepers, Cpl Mick Rainey was awarded the Military Cross - one of the first NCOs to be awarded this prestigious decoration after it ceased to be exclusively an officer's award.

(Left) In stark contrast to the summer months, the winters in Bosnia are cruel, with temperatures dropping to -40 degrees C. This photograph shows section vehicles of C Coy, 1st Bn, The Royal Highland Fusiliers, who succeeded the Poachers for Grapple 5. The wind chill factor to the driver and turret crew is significant, notwithstanding the cold airflow being channelled past the driver's position to the troop compartment. While the driver has the warmth of the engine beside him there is no heating in the rear, where even the constant use of the boiling vessel has minimal effect in the depths of a Bosnian winter.

Despite the declaration of a general ceasefire on Christmas Eve 1994 there was no reduction in effort by British forces, and 1 RHF used the opportunity to find new routes through their area of responsibility . With the usual metal stanchions to protect the turret crews from wires across the track, these Warriors are fitted with winter tracks which have steel cleats to give increased grip in icy conditions. Although they do little damage to tarmac roads they do tend to churn up unprepared surfaces, and are not overly popular with the locals, whose roads can be churned into muddy quagmires. The leading vehicle has the British Army registration number 36KG02 and its bridging classification of 30 tonnes on the lower hull front Chobham armour panel; above is an orange rectangle which indicates that the vehicle is insured against third party liability under the auspices of the United Nations.

(**Above**) At 0800 hours on 4 May 1995, 1st Bn, The Devonshire and Dorset Regiment (the old 11th, 39th and 54th of Foot) assumed the mantle of BRITBAT 1 for Operation Grapple 6. Within weeks relations between the UN and the Bosnian Serbs had worsened dramatically, culminating in the first NATO airstrikes against the Serbs; they retaliated by taking UN hostages, including 33 Welch Fusiliers of BRITBAT 2 from Gorazde and an RAF Regiment UN Military Observer. In response to this crisis Lt Gen Sir Rupert Smith, the UNPROFOR commander, instituted a theatre reserve force: 1 D & D was reconfigured as a rapid reaction force supported by artillery and armoured engineer units, to become Task Force Alpha of the Multi-National Brigade. Task Force Bravo was based on 2eme Régiment Étranger d'Infanterie (2 REI), the armoured infantry regiment of the French Foreign Legion.

Here, the FV511 of B Coy commander fires its 30mm Rarden during a live firing exercise at Lipa on 26 June 1995 during preparations for its role with Task Force Alpha. On 23 July it deployed to Mt Igman on Operation Pegasus to protect the 105mm Light Guns of 19th Regt RA bombarding Serbian positions. Warriors were next deployed to Mt Igman late in August; and on the 30th the long-awaited NATO air campaign against the Bosnian Serbs began, together with a sustained two-day bombardment by French and British artillery. The Warriors of 1 D & D added their firepower to the proceedings - not least 5 Plt of B Coy, in what was called 'Sgt Baxter's War of Attrition'. One observer remarked, 'Not even an A-10 fired *that* amount of ammunition …'

(**Opposite top**) An FV512 Warrior MCRV recovers a section vehicle. Of particular note, this MCRV of C Coy is in the standard British camouflage of green and black while its 'customer' is still in UN white; C Coy was the first to repaint its vehicles when 1 D & D was reconfigured as Task Force Alpha - a unit with a combat mission. After some initial mutual wariness between 1 D & D and 2 REI the two units soon formed a strong working relationship, which proved so successful that the CO of 1 D & D was made an honorary private first class of the Legion.

As a typical example of a BRITBAT tour on Operation Grapple, during their six months in country 1 D & D consumed 148,874 compo rations; used 13,000 toilet rolls; drove 359,705km; wore out 742 track pads, and changed 113 Warrior track sections.

(**Right**) The coldest recorded temperature on Mt Igman during the previous winter was -57

degrees C; the turret crew of callsign Three Two Charlie wear Arctic face masks as their Warrior of the Milan Platoon of 2nd Battalion, The Light Infantry negotiates a track on Mt Igman in the first week of November 1995. At the outset of Operation Grapple 7, A Coy, 2 LI continued in the rapid reaction role within the Multi-National Brigade, and supported Operation Pegasus in the relief of Sarajevo. The Milan Warriors are part of the Milan Plt of D or Fire Support Coy, whose assets are customarily divided among the rifle companies so that each can operate independently; Coy HQ are normally given tasks peculiar to Operation Grapple, e.g. battle group liaison or co-ordinating G5 humanitarian and infrastructure support. Note that this driver has his hatch in the 'umbrella' position for better vision but without impediment to the main armament.

(Opposite top) Throughout autumn 1995 intense military and political pressure on the Bosnian Serbs and the Federation culminated in the Dayton agreement of 21 November, which for the first time heralded the prospect of a lasting ceasefire in war-ravaged Bosnia. Within weeks UNPROFOR was superseded by IFOR, the Peace Implementation Force, with a much more robust mandate to enforce the terms of the agreement. With it came a change of codenames, and Operation Grapple became Operation Resolute. All forces sported new markings on the warpaint which replaced UN white; the most obvious was 'IFOR' in large white capitals, and the inverted chevron worn as the mutual recognition sign of Coalition forces during the Gulf War.

Here, the crew of the FV511 of the company commander of B Coy, 2 LI prepare for a patrol. With the change of mandate national flags returned in abundance. The cleats of the winter track are shown to advantage in this photograph. Note the vehicle name above the chevron: the battle honour BAZENTIN recalls the Somme offensive of 1916. Left of the yellow Zero Bravo callsign a roll of razor wire is lashed to the engine oil drip tray on the hull front.

(Left) Warrior is armed with a Royal Ordnance 30mm L21A1 Rarden cannon with a 7.62mm L94A1 chain gun mounted co-axially to the left. The Rarden is a recoil-operated, self-loading weapon firing single shots or bursts of up to six rounds when loaded with two three-round clips; during firing engagements the driver keeps a count of how many rounds have been fired and tells the turret crew accordingly. Spent cases are ejected forwards through the gun mantlet so, because the firing mechanism is totally enclosed, no toxic fumes can contaminate the turret space. Maximum range is 4,000m; a typical engagement would take place at 800-1,500m, at which distances the Rarden is capable of penetrating all AFVs of a similar class to Warrior when firing L14A2 APDS-T ammunition. Although effective, the Rarden is now somewhat long in the tooth, with no capability for firing on the move, and like all weapon systems it has its foibles.

With the mailed fist shoulder patch of 20th Armd Bde recalling that of the old 6th Armd Div of World War II, this Warrior commander is loading a three-round clip into the cannon, which he has to do left-handed because of his position in the turret. Similarly the Rarden has to be charged by the cocking handle visible below the yellow-tipped High Explosive round; this is tiring for right-handers, requiring about a dozen turns of increasing severity.

(Above) Much of IFOR's success (so far) has been due to a serious show of force in support of the Dayton agreement, delivering the message that the NATO-commanded contingents are ready to use their firepower if obliged to do so. A welter of new military acronyms have appeared: units patrol the ACFL in the ZOS between the IEBL of the FWF - the Agreed Cease Fire Lines in the Zones Of Separation between the Inter-Entity Boundary Lines of the Former Warring Factions ... . To this end the British Army has committed further forces including Challenger I MBTs; Warrior companies are now attached to tank squadrons or vice versa to form armour- or infantry-heavy battle groups, whose mobility and firepower are sufficient to dissuade even the most recalcitrant warlord from breaking the peace. During Operation Resolute II the Warrior unit was 1st Battalion, The Worcestershire and Sherwood Foresters Regiment. These section vehicles of the Woofers' C Coy are on patrol from Camp Sherwood in the area known as the 'Anvil' during the tense period leading up to the elections of September 1996.

(Above) As the successor to IFOR, SFOR or Stabilisation Force continues to keep the peace under the codename Operation Lodestar. Lately the use of Warrior for patrolling has significantly diminished, since its appearance is deemed to give too aggressive a message for the current situation. Many patrols are now conducted by Land Rovers and other light vehicles, which also inflict less damage on roads and tracks. The Roman numerals XIX on its trackguard identify this Warrior as belonging to the old 19th Regiment of Foot - The Green Howards (Alexandra, Princess of Wales's Own Yorkshire Regiment). It is deployed here on a joint patrol with a Muslim militiaman; such patrols are conducted with representatives of each faction to show the impartiality of SFOR. While fulfilling this task with their usual professionalism, British troops take a somewhat jaundiced view of them: invariably the other parties fail to appear or, if they do, the only thing joint about the proceedings is what the locals are smoking.

(Opposite top) An important element of the reinforcement of British forces in Bosnia with the creation of IFOR was the deployment of 18 AS90 155mm self-propelled howitzers divided between three six-gun batteries: two composite batteries (17/159 and 127/16) of 26th Regt RA, and 52 Bty from 4th Regiment RA. With a range of 30km and the capacity to fire three rounds in ten seconds per gun, they massively enhanced the firepower of the all-arms battle groups of Multi-National Division South West, whose area of operations extends approximately 180 x 200 kilometers. Any engagement would be controlled by the attached Warrior Battery Command Vehicle, shown here in IFOR colours, with the AS90s in the background soon after their arrival.

In its first operational deployment the AS90 has proved a most capable weapons system but, as always, some interesting tactical problems have arisen. Not the least of these was the need for a coherent chain of command - during the early days the Gunners received orders from eight separate superior headquarters. The weather has also had a significant effect, with temperature variations of up to 34 degrees C in less than 12 hours. In the arcane art of gunnery this represents a difference in range for a 155mm projectile, at even low charges, of 100m - a considerable factor when infantrymen on the ground are in need of close artillery support.

(Right) Captain Richard Sutton of 4th Regt RA acts as the Forward Observation Officer in a Warrior MAOV (or in Gunner parlance, Warrior OPV - Observation Post Vehicle) during a firepower demonstration on the Glamoc ranges on 9 April 1997. He is feeding data into the Battlefield Artillery Target Engagement System, which is the principal computer for controlling the fire of AS90 batteries. Below BATES, his hand is obscuring the remote display for the thermal imaging system of his Pilkington PE Osprey combined day, thermal and laser designating sight. The Warrior MAOV can accommodate a crew of six: driver; commander and observer in the turret; and three men in the back to operate the extensive communications equipment and the MSTAR battlefield surveillance and target acquisition radar. For maximum range, MSTAR can be raised on a mast at the rear of the vehicle, or can even be sited remotely should the tactical situation demand. The M in MSTAR stands for Manportable, but not everyone would agree with this designation.

(Below) Airburst smoke rounds fired by AS90 155mm self-propelled howitzers explode in unison on the Resolute Barbara range at Glamoc during a firepower demonstration by Multi-National Division South West. Such displays are held periodically to impress upon local warlords and representatives of the 'Former Warring Factions' SFOR's capability to bring down overwhelming firepower anywhere within the divisional area of operations should they choose to disrupt the fragile peace. In a concerted orchestra of weapons systems, American, British, Canadian, Czech, Dutch and Malaysian troops provide a formidable spectacle of

co-ordinated direct and indirect fire. These include Challenger MBTs, Scimitar CVR(T)s and Warriors of the British contingent; Canadian 81mm mortars in Wolf LAVs, and TOW under armour from M981; Czech 30mm cannon fire from their BMP-2s; Dutch Leopard 2 MBTs firing 120mm main armament; Malaysians in Condor APCs with 20mm Oerlikons; and US Apache attack helicopters, reminding observers of the utter devastation they wrought upon the Iraqi army during the Gulf War of 1991.

In addition, the dismounted infantry contribute their not inconsiderable firepower including LAW; TOW and Dragon ATGW; Sustained Fire (SF) machine guns; and any other

infantry weapon from grenade launcher to sniper rifle that the troops can lay their hands on - they much enjoy the prodigal allocation of ammunition that such demonstrations allow, courtesy of the United Nations. Since much of the ammunition is generally almost time - expired, it would otherwise have to be withdrawn from service, and using it up in this way provides invaluable experience for the troops on the ground. Here, a Warrior section vehicle of 2nd Battalion, The Royal Regiment of Fusiliers stands guard next to an infantry weapons pit to mark its position to other players in this firepower demonstration.

Warrior development

(Right) Following the Gulf War, the Kuwaiti Armed Forces conducted comparative trials between a hot weather version of Warrior and the Bradley M2 Infantry Fighting Vehicle. In August 1993 the Desert Warrior was selected and an agreement was signed for the production of 254 vehicles, the first of which was delivered on schedule in October 1994. The most obvious of its significant differences from the British Army version is the American Delco Defence Systems Operations two-man turret, mounting a fully stabilised

McDonnell-Douglas M242 25mm chain gun together with a pair of Hughes TOW ATGW launchers externally. Desert Warrior can fire its main armament accurately when on the move, while TOW can destroy enemy AFVs out to a range of 3,750 metres. Other notable enhancements are the full width Chobham armour panel on the front hull; a combined air conditioning and NBC filtration unit; thermal imaging night sights; GPS navigation equipment; and modified trackguards to minimise the dust thrown up. Desert Warrior is now fully operational with the Kuwaiti Land Forces, which have fielded a total of four battalions within the 26th Al Soor Brigade. (GKN Defence)

(**Below**) With a Perkins CV8 TCA V8/Allison X-300-4B powerpack painted in its distinctive duck-egg blue in the foreground, Desert Warriors are assembled at the GKN Defence factory at Telford in Shropshire. The last Desert Warrior was delivered on schedule in October 1997, and with it the Warrior production line was closed. (GKN Defence)

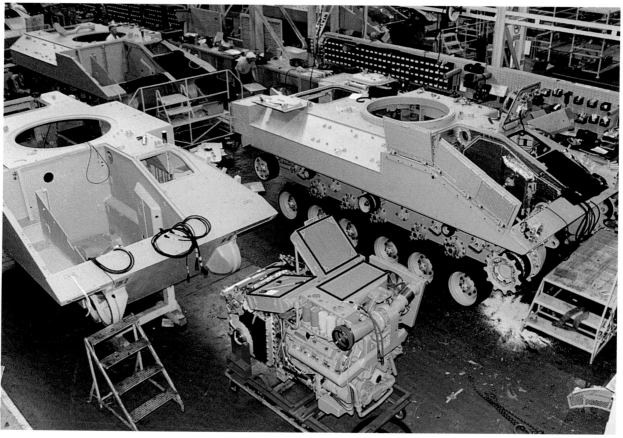

(Above) In a dramatic company photograph GKN Defence unveils the latest variant of Warrior, which is configured specifically for the reconnaissance role. It operates in advance of an armoured battle group and collects intelligence through a sophisticated array of sensors. Designated Warrior Reconnaissance, the vehicle shares the same turret system as Desert Warrior, but the hull is shorter, with the deletion of one roadwheel station. With a crew of three comprising the driver plus two in the turret, there is provision in the rear for a fourth crew member to monitor the various sensors. With the same powerpack as a standard Warrior, the recce version has a high power-to-weight ratio providing high speed and agility. Its thermal, radar and acoustic signatures have been significantly reduced to decrease the risk of being detected on the battlefield. The doctrine of the British Army has been to acquire intelligence by stealth rather than firepower, although the latter is well served by the latest Delco turret system. (GKN Defence)

(Opposite top) Posed in its distinctive black livery, the Warrior Reconnaissance features a mast-mounted, multi-spectral surveillance system incorporating a daylight camera, thermal imaging, laser rangefinder, and a battlefield surveillance radar. The information acquired by all these sensors is processed through a Fully Integrated Battle Management System to pass back information to the force commander in real time. With its enhanced armour package covering the whole front and hull sides, stabilised gun and TOW launchers Warrior Reconnaissance represents a significant advance in terms of mobility, firepower and protection over existing vehicles, while its sophisticated sensors and thermal imaging sights for each crew member allow it to operate on a 24-hour basis in all weather conditions.(Simon Dunstan)

(Opposite centre) Although the Warrior production line is now closed, GKN Defence has developed a version for export incorporating many new features.

Known as Warrior 30, it mounts a Delco Defence Systems all electric two-man turret armed with a fully stabilised 30mm Bushmaster II cannon made by the Boeing Company (which has merged with McDonnell-Douglas, the original producer of Bushmaster cannons). Warrior 30 has been offered to the Swiss Army, which has a requirement for 310 vehicles to replace its ageing M113 APCs. In an open competition, Warrior 30 will be pitted against the Swedish Hagglunds CV 9030, which is also armed with the Bushmaster II cannon, and the German KUKAM12 - a development of the Marder. All these vehicles will be evaluated in Switzerland during 1998 with a decision to be taken late in 1999 and deliveries to run between 2002 and 2006. (Simon Dunstan)

(Opposite bottom) As a further private venture, GKN Defence has produced a utility variant of Warrior which may be configured to undertake numerous roles on the battlefield. With its vertical hull sides - unlike those of the standard Warrior, which are chamfered at the top - the utility version has greater internal volume in the rear compartment. Among the variants envisaged for Utility Warrior are logistic resupply; mortar carrier; armoured ambulance; guided missile carrier, and command post. This Utility Warrior is configured in the latter role and is fitted out with a comprehensive array of the latest military electronics, including the Aerosystems Apache planning station; GIAT Industries FINDERS battle management system (Fast Information, Navigation, Decision and Reporting System, as fitted to the Leclerc MBT); RACAL Bowman PDI radios (Bowman being one of the contenders for the British Army's next generation tactical radio family); and various computers such as the Lynwood Genesis - these electronic systems being more expensive than the vehicle itself. Although this example has Chobham armour protecting the hull front only, production models can be fitted with a complete appliqué armour package as on Warrior 30. (Simon Dunstan)

Warrior Reconnaissance

Warrior 30

Utility Warrior

Warrior has now been fully operational with the British Army for ten years, and has proved to be a most effective machine. Most types of AFV have idiosyncracies which colour the user's opinion; but Warrior is one of those rare beasts that is highly reliable and versatile, as has been proven in both the Gulf and Bosnian theatres. However, as the time approaches for a mid-life enhancement programme

there is the opportunity for some essential improvements. Thermal imaging sights are the most desirable, followed by a fully stabilised main armament replacement for the Rarden - a serious contender being the innovative Anglo-French 45mm CT2000 Cased Telescopic Weapon. Whatever is decided, 'the wagon' will certainly soldier on for many years to come in the ranks of British battle groups.

(Back cover) With his company flag flying high, the officer commanding B Company, 1st Royal Highland Fusiliers observes his men from his FV511 Warrior command vehicle during Exercise Uhlan Eagle 96. Command vehicles are commonly referred to as 'Five Elevens', whereas the 'FV510 Combat Vehicle Personnel, Tracked 30mm Gun Warrior' - to give it its full designation - is usually referred to as a 'section

vehicle' or by crews simply as 'the wagon'. Just visible here is the Uhlan Eagle exercise 'zap' stuck to the commander's sight cover. In the background is a Warrior fitted with a Milan firing post as an Anti-Tank Guided Weapon Carrier in the battalion Fire Support Company. This variant was first introduced during the Gulf War of 1991, when the Milan firing post was mounted on top of the turret. (Simon Dunstan)